ENTJ: 33 Secrets From The Life of an ENTJ

By Diana Jackson

Contents

ENTJ: Extraverted, Intuitive, Thinking, Judging

1. At their best in a leadership position

Positive: There are leaders and then there are ENTJs, the personalities most comfortable and effective in leadership positions. And it's not that they like to lead for the thrill of being in charge or getting to control everyone – ENTJs are logical, thoughtful visionaries who truly have what it takes to propel progress.

Negative: Naturally, ENTJs in subordinate positions can be seen bristling at the prospect of someone else telling them what to do, especially if they perceive that person to be of lesser intelligence. They'll be the ones to openly challenge the person in charge, causing some people's jaws to drop with the boldness of their critiques.

In Relationships: ENTJs must definitely take care not to get controlling in their relationships, so it's important that they find people with stiff back-bones, who aren't going to take orders. In any case, that's the kind of person the ENTJ likes: fiery, passionate and with a mind of his or her own. Then they can learn to compromise together.

At Work: For all the positives and negatives that come with being a natural born leader, the workplace is the location where the ENTJ's most obvious talents can spread their wings and fly. If they don't start at the top, well, they certainly work their way there, clobbering all the incompetents who get in their way.

2. Views life as a challenge

Positive: People who consistently view life as a challenge are consistently becoming better versions of themselves while bettering the world around them. For a certainty, a competitive spirit and a great deal of ambition will take you far in the world, and with the ENTJ's natural assertiveness and courage, they can accomplish everything they dream.

Negative: Sometimes, though – and others around the ENTJ can see it best – these types just need to relax. Making a competition out of who can use the public restroom faster is a sign that someone needs to take a vacation and slow down. Enjoying life in a peaceful way is not wasting time.

In Relationships: Whether it's winning over someone or constantly surprising and delighting the one they are with, ENTJs can get competitive even in relationships. Certainly, the gauntlet has been thrown if they find themselves in direct competition with someone else for the same person. Let the battle of wits and strategy begin.

At Work: A lot of ENTJs end up doing white-collar work, like running businesses or practicing law, and their outlook on life is readily handy in these two fields especially. Any businessman knows that every year has to see the company doing better, while lawyers take on case assignments to argue for people they know are guilty. That's a work challenge.

3. Easily and quickly grasps complexities

Positive: If you have ever had a friend who had to have everything spelled out before they understood the situation, you can appreciate the ENTJ's talent for surmising a situation with one glance around the room or by asking only two or three pointed questions.

Negative: If ENTJs pick up on subtleties and understand what is going on faster than everyone else, they're also bored waiting for others to catch up, and they can get a tad snotty about it. As highly expressive types who aren't afraid to have their voices heard, those voices can sometimes imply that others are slow or dumb.

In Relationships: ENTJs are interesting when it comes to relationships, because while they can understand the complexities of why someone can't date them – a tangled history, for instance – they truly believe the choice is a simple one. Either you care about them and want to be with them, or you don't.

At Work: Part of the reason ENTJs can be seen to rise to the upper ranks of whatever field they're in is because they are so quick and so intelligent. If figuring stuff out is a race, they're the mental Usain Bolts, and that kind of speed is impressive and worthy of promotion.

4. Has a confident and forceful personality

Positive: ENTJs can be forceful to the point of obnoxious, but one thing is for certain: they're not the types who get ignored in restaurants or talked down to by sales clerks. In fact, their confidence in who they are often gives them an authority so palpable that they don't have to open their mouths at all. One look will do.

Negative: As mentioned, ENTJs can be confident and forceful to the point where people don't want to be around them or immediately decide they don't like them. This can cause the ENTJ to burn a lot of bridges before they even cross the river, losing them powerful potential allies and friends.

In Relationships: Being pursued by an ENTJ is one of life's most thrilling chases, like something you'd see on the nature channels on TV. ENTJ men in particular are like the quintessential romance novel heroes, the men accustomed to getting whatever – and whoever – they want, no holds barred.

At Work: Even as subordinates in the workplace, ENTJs can be singled out for success by virtue of their willingness to put themselves out there and be seen. Such is their confidence that critique or even criticism doesn't faze them; in fact, they absorb the suggestion that they can do better and use it to become more powerful.

5. Does very well academically

Positive: Whatever the subject, ENTJs are seen as intellectually gifted from a young age. Precocious and curious, willing to put in the hard work that is generally required to obtain good grades, these types always have the right answer, and not just in concrete areas like science and math. They are surprisingly insightful in subjects like literature and art history, too.

Negative: ENTJs' teachers might try to get them to sign up to be tutors, but this type just doesn't have the inclination in them, the way Feeling types might. The way they see it, their intelligence and superior academic performance is all for themselves, and tutoring would require them to waste time that could be spent doing something more productive for their future.

In Relationships: It stands to reason then that ENTJs who meet their significant others in school are not going to fall for the guy or gal who requires tutoring, but are going to gravitate toward the other brilliant minds in the class, perhaps even viewing them through the lens of playful competition before realizing the chemistry and attraction is there.

At Work: Grades aren't everything, but the ENTJ's academic transcripts are definitely something, the kind of well-rounded records which show straight A's and tons of impressive extracurriculars – exactly the tool you need to get into a good college and then get a great job.

6. Is very active and engaged in relationships

Positive: ENTJs might surprise people with how deeply they care about the people close to them (certainly, those whom they don't care for so much feel the sting of their disregard), but make no mistake: while they might not be Feeling types, they feel intense love for their family and wild passion for their mates.

Negative: ENTJs love the people close to them just as much as they love to succeed, and when the two come to a loggerheads, it can be intensely uncomfortable for the ENTJ to have to choose. They are not naturally disposed toward making decisions based on the feelings of others, but they don't want to hurt their loved ones.

In Relationships: With their mates, ENTJs are energetic and love to take them out to do things, whether it's physical activities like beautiful sunset hikes or an expensive meal at a new restaurant. What's more, you can leave all the planning to the ENTJ, who isn't bothered at all by making the arrangements and reservations (it also gives them the chance to plan little surprises).

At Work: ENTJs don't necessarily get close to the people with whom they work and collaborate, but they do understand the importance of a strong working relationship, especially if it's a desirable client or colleague. So while they themselves might not remember the client's daughter's birthday, they will definitely make sure their assistant or receptionist remembers to send over a gift for the occasion.

7. Focused on furthering their own ambitions

Positive: The ENTJ's vision for the world is usually progressive, technologically advanced and culturally sophisticated, so it's difficult to criticize this type for always seeking to further their ambitions. If you can see where they are coming from – or more importantly, where they want to go – it's difficult not to be seduced by their fantasies, too.

Negative: Look closely, though, and you'll see that ENTJs imagine themselves as the puppeteers who pull all the strings, the very masters of power – the spiders sitting at the middle of their masterful web. And they can be insensitive, if not downright ruthless, when it comes to obtaining their goals.

In Relationships: ENTJs do care for true love, but if they can have both affection *and* a partner whose ambitions match their own, someone who brings their own unique talent for climbing the ladder one rung at a time, then that would be their ideal. Why not attain the heights of success with an equal partner standing by your side?

At Work: Make no mistake: for ENTJs, business is business (is business). Even if you pet sat for them for a week while they were on vacation in Maldives, if they have to pulverize you professionally to get where they want to go, consider yourself obliterated. It doesn't make them popular, but it sure does make them successful.

8. Has a passion for the sciences

Positive: ENTJs bring an intimidating and exciting mix of creativity and imagination, plus a thoroughly grounded understanding of the rules of science to their interest in topics like physics and chemistry and biology. Whether they pursue it professionally or merely dabble as a hobbyist, ENTJs are capable of some outstanding discoveries.

Negative: The ENTJ will sink a lot of their spare time into playing around with a robot or building a high-tech computer, when what they really need to do is practice relating to others and not offending people. While their passion for science is admirable, the area of their personality that most needs work is in their own hearts.

In Relationships: The ENTJ requires a rather forgiving partner, if only because they are bound to abandon them for dinner with old college buddies, where they can spend hours picking apart the physics projects they used to assemble together back in the day. Best if the ENTJ's mate has a lot of hobbies of his or her own.

At Work: Quite a few ENTJs end up in the sciences, usually in pioneering tech fields like Steve Jobs did before his passing. A good practical background in science helps, but ENTJs are definitely ideas folk, the guys and gals who take scientific fact and then imagine all the various ways that it can be manipulated.

9. Completes the tasks they are given

Positive: One of the most important traits for any successful human being is the ability to endure and persevere. Refusing to give up displays determination and ambition, and the ENTJ has those qualities in spades, setting their minds to the tasks at hand and relentlessly pursuing them to the best of their abilities.

Negative: When faced with a moral dilemma which stands in the way of him or her completing an important task, the ENTJ will almost undoubtedly choose to stay the course, even if it means horrible consequences for others. Each of us has free will, and ENTJs choose to exercise that right in a way that occasionally borders on the cruel. And sadly, it almost always comes back to haunt them.

In Relationships: A lot of people have homes that look a bit ramshackle, because someone started a home improvement project but never finished it. Not so the ENTJ's living quarters, much to the delight of their spouses, who can always count on their partners to do the job right, as efficiently as possible.

At Work: It doesn't take long for ENTJs to reach the position where they have climbed higher than their own bosses on the corporate ladder, and that is because they show an absolute reliability and perseverance. The guy or lady who is willing to jump onto a plane, at their own expense, and fly halfway around the world to hand-deliver a report is the person who gets promotions.

10. Comfortable around others in social situations

Positive: ENTJs might not be the friendliest sorts, but they are no shrinking violets, and if the topic is one they are interested in, they are downright boisterous and fun to be around. Their extraversion is normally functions like a megaphone for calling other people out, but like other extraverts, they truly enjoy being around people.

Negative: Without much Feeling going on, however, the ENTJ can get too comfortable and may push conversations in uncomfortable directions or say things that are just horribly inappropriate. This has the effect of pushing potential friends away, if not sending them running in the opposite direction.

In Relationships: Particularly when ENTJs are among friends and family, they can relax and be at their most amiable and personable. Their partners likely love this side of them, and enjoy going out with friends for dinner, drinks and dancing, letting them enjoy the atmosphere and enjoy cutting loose for a night in happy companionship.

At Work: While everyone else in the board room might be on tenterhooks, the ENTJ is completely confident and comfortable, no matter if they are presenting something to the big wigs of the company or are the big wig themselves. Are they oblivious to everyone else's discomfort? No, and the wicked thing is, they might even be enjoying it.

11. Thinks innovatively and originally

Positive: If there is ever a situation which calls for creativity and originality, the ENTJ is an exception go-to person to have on-call. Among friends and family they quickly gain a reputation for problem-solving that is both innovative and logical, while keeping long-term goals in mind.

Negative: Unfortunately, ENTJs have a difficult time harnessing their creative thinking powers for more short-term or practical problems, like a blown tire on the highway. While they would suggest a great low-profile mechanic who sells top-of-the-line tires at good prices for the future, it doesn't help the friend who is stranded on the side of the road on a burning hot day with any immediacy.

In Relationships: Once the ENTJ has found the person with whom he or she plans to spend the right of their lives, the fun can really start. While ENTJs are methodical and detail-oriented, they tend also to envision a future that is full of creature comforts for themselves and their families, and they will go to work, strategizing a lifestyle that enables them to work hard and play hard.

12. Makes quick and decisive judgments

Positive: Whether it's over people or situations, ENTJs put much stock in making a decision – dilly-dallying over the proper course is so not their style. Thanks to this part of their personality, they waste the least amount of time – something the rest of us would do well to emulate more in our lives.

Negative: Because they are so thoughtful, analytical and thorough, it's rare for ENTJs to make a bad decision, but when someone chooses their options quickly, as a rule in their life, they are bound to leap to a bad choice eventually. In fact, ENTJs can become so arrogant (or self-assured) in their decision-making that they get sloppy.

In Relationships: One of the great things about the ENTJ in relationships is that he or she does not leave people hanging, nor lead people on if they aren't interested. This is a really bum move that a lot of people will pull when they think they are being "nice" by not hurting someone's feelings right away. The ENTJ spares everyone by just yanking the band aid off quickly.

At Work: Effective leaders know when someone isn't pulling their weight and they take quick action to mitigate that person's negative effect. For the ENTJ, they might offer a rare bit of leniency and give the weak link a second chance, but beyond that there is little mercy. Those who cannot pull their weight get the ax.

13. Always views situations with a "take charge" attitude

Positive: In the ENTJ's mind, there is no situation that could not be bettered if they were in charge, and to be fair, a lot of the time they are correct. They are not only visionaries who burn up with their dreams for how the world can be, they are supremely gifted organizers and flawlessly fierce logicians.

Negative: Sometimes, situations already have a leader. For instance, in times of natural disaster, there are people with degrees in crisis management, who work with local authorities every day to ensure that crisis plans are up-to-date and effective. When the ENTJ comes barging to the front, trying to impose their will as they see fit, they can make a bad matter worse.

In Relationships: More subordinate types might vibe better with the ENTJ in a relationship, but it would be better for this personality type to partner off with someone who displays equal amounts of leadership, if only so that both sides can learn the fine art of compromise, knowledge that they can apply to other parts of their lives to great effect.

At Work: There is nothing a boss likes to see more than a self-starter, and that is definitely what the ENTJ is. Without being told to do so, they instinctively know what the best, logical thing to accomplish is, and they will not only set themselves to do it, they can ably organize their fellow coworkers in a coordinated effort (spearheaded by themselves, of course).

14. Focused on their careers

Positive: ENTJs have high expectations for themselves, and may have grown up with a lot expected out of them from others. There is nothing wrong with ambition, particularly when the ENTJ's ambition tends to benefit all of us, at least indirectly. So if the ENTJ is focused on his or her career, it's mostly to the good.

Negative: If ever there were a workaholic, the ENTJ is it. This type takes their work with them wherever they go, and may even suffer health issues as a result of the stress. Sleeplessness, weight gain, irritation and even more serious matters like heart disease are caused by stress, which intense focus on one's career can exacerbate.

In Relationships: If there is anyone who can convince the ENTJ to just take a week off and enjoy tropical weather, it's their mate. The ENTJ's partner does, however, have his or her work cut out for them, and it's not uncommon for this type to sneak in a conference call in the Bahamas.

At Work: ENTJs are capable of some pretty ruthless acts to get themselves to the top, it must be said. This isn't everyone's style, but it is the way of the world, and ENTJs don't just play the game – they make their own rules without telling anyone else. It is to their credit, however, that they tend to achieve "the impossible" – or rather, what was impossible before they tried.

15. Fully self-confident

Positive: ENTJs don't need others telling them how great they are – they know. Which isn't to say that they go around boasting to everyone; it just shows, naturally, in the way they comport themselves, oftentimes with great dignity and poise. Even in the most chaotic of times, ENTJs walk around as if their feet don't touch the ground.

Negative: Despite the fact that they might not be the boastful sort, ENTJ self-confidence can manifest itself into arrogant behavior that alienates more people than it impresses. After all, actions speak louder than words, and even if the ENTJ doesn't mean to be rude or insensitive as a result of their confidence, they can be perceived as such.

In Relationships: These types don't necessarily need partners for moral support, but they do crave companionship, the same as anyone else. Their self-confidence can repel as many would-be romantic interests as it attracts; it's all a matter of what the other person likes.

At Work: The ENTJ who occupies the lowest run of their career field nonetheless walks into work every day as if they own the place. In a way, that's part of attaining success – projecting an aura of confidence and poise that seems to suggest they are not at the top yet, but soon will be.

16. Places importance on personal hygiene

Positive: Neat, trim and pulled-together – these are the physical qualities that the ENTJ most frequently embodies, and it contributes to their overall aura of confidence. You will never catch this personality type running out to the store in sweatpants – they always make the effort to look their best.

Negative: ENTJs can be difficult because a lot of the qualities that they themselves embody, they likewise expect others to follow suit in prioritizing. But using the sweatpants example, plenty of people run to the store in their sweats, a hat to cover their unwashed hair and, for the ladies, no make-up – and there's nothing wrong with that, but the ENTJ can get a little judgmental.

In Relationships: Significant others of the ENTJ will be pleasantly surprised, particularly when it comes to the males, who have a reputation for bad hygiene (more so than women). Instead, both sexes place a high premium on appearances, and that includes eating well and exercising regularly as part of their daily life.

At Work: For some people, and particularly for ENTJs, part of being successful is looking successful. Those who are starting at the bottom will present themselves to the world, trussed up for the success they desire, and those who have already climbed the heights make their authority more palpable by looking clean and well-groomed at all times.

17. Seeks out attention and fame

Positive: ENTJs know that being talked about means that you're relevant – and pretty much all press is good press. If being noticed means that the ENTJ's business or authority is more widely recognized, then that is a-ok with them, and there is a good chance that in order to enhance their prestige they will seek out photo ops and public appearances.

Negative: Actually, sometimes bad press is just that – bad, and encouraging it does damage rather than enhances public recognition, but the ENTJ can be rather stubborn on this account. It can take a lot before the ENTJ finally acknowledges that their reputation has been badly damaged because they allowed their fame to become monstrous.

In Relationships: It can be extremely difficult for the significant others and spouses of INTJs to be forced to live in the public eye, along with their partner. Of course, some people welcome it, but many would prefer not to be followed by gossip magazine paps who are trying to learn all the intimate details of their lives.

At Work: At least INTJs should try to keep the press and their fame focused on their work, because that is where they are usually succeeding with flying colors. Many of these types will find, however, that a publicist or PR team is necessary to keep the media circus around their fame to a minimum.

18. Wishes to be constantly busy or occupied

Positive: Although the ENTJ's pace might seem awfully frantic to outsiders who are accustomed to a more relaxed lifestyle, constantly being busy or occupied suits this personality type to a T. They have vast stores of energy, and if they have nothing to do the ENTJ is a lot like a bored puppy – gleefully destructive. Better for us all if we just sit back and let them do, do, do.

Negative: ENTJs practically move at the speed of light, their bodies racing almost as fast as their formidable minds, and you have to either run at their pace or get the heck out of the way – because they will shed you like a snake's skin if you slow them down. It's an efficient way to live, but not the kindest.

In Relationships: ENTJ partners, if they aren't part of their mate's whirl of activity, can feel like they're still single at times, eating microwaved dinners alone in the kitchen. This is because the ENTJ's many occupations tend to be work-related, so even if their partner wanted to accompany them, they couldn't. These types should clearly define personal and professional activities and carve out time for each.

At Work: For a certainty, the chief activity in the ENTJ's life is the upward ascension of their professional status, so while they might be caught skiing or playing tennis, that's only an aperitif between the main courses: work-related activity that sees them managing, brainstorming and networking.

19. Actively seeks problems to solve

Positive: ENTJs aren't naturally what you would call humanitarians, but oftentimes inefficiency accompanies social injustice, and these personality types are logical enough and keen enough to recognize that. So while their main goal in seeking out problems to solve might not be first and foremost to help the oppressed, they end up doing so anyway (and perhaps learning a thing or two along the way).

Negative: ENTJs aren't naturally what you would call nosy, either, but they do have a way of inserting themselves into situations where their input perhaps isn't welcome (or needed). They do tend to assume that their way is the right way, and that everyone should be grateful for their advice, but that is not the case.

In Relationships: Somewhere along the line the ENTJ's partner may say, "Stop! Stop trying to fix something that isn't broken!" This can include anything from a fridge that is actually running just fine (although the ENTJ insists it's not as cold today as it was yesterday) to issues with the children, who are just being kids.

At Work: The workplace is a horse of a different color, because there are always underlying issues that need to be addressed. A business, for instance, has a million little problems that can grow bigger – and it can take you by surprise if you aren't vigilant. ENTJs might seem like they are looking for trouble outside of work, but within the confines of their careers their watchfulness is a huge advantage.

20. Considers things from a long-range perspective

Positive: In all aspects of their lives, the ENTJ is first and foremost an Intuitive thinker, clever, theoretical and always looking to the future. While there is a place for Sensing types in the world (of course), Intuitives drive progress forward by starting in one place in time but planning for the years to come.

Negative: There are always things to consider in the here and now, however, and the details can be lost to the ENTJ, who is so busy plotting for whatever is to come months or years down the road that they miss the present. Long-term planning is good, of course, but it is not everything, and ENTJs need to slow down and look around themselves.

In Relationships: Once the ENTJ has found a good match they are most likely going to start thinking about where it could lead. If they take a rather scientific approach to analyzing their significant other's advantages and disadvantages, strengths and weaknesses, it's only because they are trying to figure out whether they have a real future with this person – something all of us can relate to.

At Work: The ENTJ is a consummate professional in all matters, and he or she plays the long game when it comes to their work. They may look inconspicuous at first, but trust in the fact that the ENTJ plants a seed one day and sees it come to fruition in the months or even years to come. Never underestimate the ENTJ – he or she is cleverer even than they let on.

21. Likes to surround themselves with people in power

Positive: The ENTJ him or herself strives to be a "person in power," so it makes sense that they seek out people who currently occupy the heights. In so doing they can ingratiate themselves among the types of people they hope to stand among one day. Those who are already at the top of their game can use the friendships and connections with other power players to further their ambitions.

Negative: There is a saying that more or less goes, "The toes you step on today may be the behinds you have to kiss tomorrow," and ENTJs would be wise to heed these words. Instead of exclusively positioning themselves among presidents and CEOs, they should take care to form connections with those of lower status – even the janitor of their building. You never know whose influence you will need.

In Relationships: Far from being threatened by a powerful partner, ENTJs are turned on in more ways than one by an equal. In fact, having another power player by their side gives them even more confidence and, truly, inspires them to achieve more, if only to impress someone whose opinion matters to them.

At Work: ENTJs know, however, that forming alliances and connections with individuals who are in the one percent of their field is still one of the wisest moves they can make in order to both climb the ladder to success and stay there at the top once they have reached the summit. It's a bit like a club, and ENTJs are sure to try and dominate even that group of over-achievers.

22. Easily irritated; impatient

Positive: There might not be a whole lot that's good about someone who is easily irritated or who feels impatient when they are forced to wait for others to catch up, but the ENTJ is at least willing to speak up and voice their irritation, rather than talking behind someone's back. Perhaps it was time for someone to point out the inefficiencies or flaws.

Negative: An important lesson that ENTJs need to learn – but rarely do – is that their lives are not more imperative or pressing than others. They need to calm down, take a few deep breaths and learn the fine art of patience when it comes to others. Not everyone is blessed with such penetrating gifts of perception, but that doesn't make them stupid or dull.

In Relationships: It could do the ENTJ a world of good to meet and date someone who makes them feel inferior (the way they do to others). Through no other path will they learn empathy, so a little tough love it must be. Once they have had a taste of what it feels like to be the "slow" one, perhaps they'll think twice before snapping at someone else.

At Work: The workplace is perhaps the worst location for the ENTJ's fit of irritation and impatience, because unfortunately they have little scruple about bringing the hammer down, hard, on their subordinates. In their minds it's a simple process of weeding the garden, but they have to be aware that they are really hurting people's feelings.

23. Dislikes mistakes and errors (especially in others)

Positive: If the ENTJ has made an error and someone can point it out in a logical and straightforward manner, they will be the first to admit that they were in the wrong, though they will find the whole matter distasteful. If someone else has made an error, they can at least take the ENTJ's critique (more likely criticism) and improve themselves.

Negative: The ENTJ's critique could be some of the harshest and most soul-killing feedback anyone ever receives, because this type does not believe in holding back when they are displeased. To further cement the ENTJ's reputation for cold-heartedness, their own mistakes are dealt with and departed from with as little fuss as possible – making them pretty obvious hypocrites at times.

In Relationships: Again, the ENTJ needs a taste of his or her own medicine if they are ever to learn about taking the high road and saying the tactful thing, rather than the bluntly honest truth. ENTJ's partners are uniquely positioned to teach them about empathy, because they are trusted and respected.

At Work: Employees and other subordinates of the ENTJ likely have high blood pressure from all the stress of pleasing their boss person, and this in turn creates a work atmosphere where people are willing to throw each other under the buss to avoid being blamed for mistakes. Perhaps the ENTJ should relax a touch and not bring out the worst in their employees.

24. Has a difficult time considering the feelings of others

Positive: Many people make poor choices because they cannot help but consider how their action will affect others, on a purely superficial level. So and so will be sad, so and so will be angry – but the fact is, people build up the consequences in their minds to be worse than the reality. But not ENTJs, who examine facts, not people's surface feelings.

Negative: There are plenty of situations, however, where a great deal of heart is necessary and showing empathy to others is the best course of action. For instance, if Grandma is sick in the hospital, telling your cousin to stop crying because it is annoying everyone is a terrible thing to do (even if it is true).

In Relationships: If the ENTJ announces to his or her family that they are packing up and moving across the country – with no prior discussion – it's not that they are trying to make everyone miserable, it's that they simply have no notion of how their actions make other people feel, because they never stop to think. Feeling types with a stiff upper lip can swoop in and do damage control here.

At Work: In some ways, the ENTJs lack of empathy is a good thing, because there are plenty of careers where impartiality and unbiased judgment are important – such as law, where defense lawyers must put aside their personal repugnancy for accused criminals and face victims' families, knowing full well their client committed the crime. It takes a special kind of person to do this; it takes an ENTJ.

25. Can be selfish

Positive: We live in a world where nothing is handed to us – if we want something, we have to take it (or plot our way to it). Random acts of kindness are just that – random, and therefore cannot be relied upon. The ENTJ who has come from nothing may exhibit a degree of selfishness in his or her life, but it is their way of getting what they want – and they do work for it.

Negative: Selfishness is selfishness, however, no matter how you dress it up, and that always implies that someone else is coming out the loser because the ENTJ is coming out ahead. And while it is great that someone can get whatever they want if they work hard, ENTJs need to learn that attaining goals at someone else's expense is not winning.

In Relationships: ENTJs can be selfish in a lot of ways when it comes to their relationships – they hoard their time for work-related activities and they can be demanding and critical while giving themselves a lot of behavioral leeway. Yet to balance this out, they are committed and sincere, to say nothing of completely honest.

At Work: ENTJs might take credit for something they didn't do, but they are more likely to simply exaggerate their role in an effort to look good, thereby hogging the spotlight (as they are wont to do) to further their climb to the top. They should be aware, however, that selfish behavior almost always falls back on the greedy individual somehow.

26. Has difficulty seeing things from other people's POV

Positive: While the ENTJ could benefit from a great deal more empathy, it is to their credit that they have such a pronounced world view of their own. This is a confident, poised personality type; they know exactly who they are and what they believe in, and they are willing to stand up for both.

Negative: Being closed off from the opinions and feelings of others – because you are certain your own are so superior – leads to blind spots and even bigotry. If want ENTPs want to run the world, they are going to have to be able to relate to everyone in the world, as opposed to thinking that everyone should change themselves to relate to one person.

In Relationships: ENTJs, bless them, could reason their way out of a parking ticket, but if they can't understand why being stood up last minute on an anniversary hurts their significant other's feelings, *fuggetaboutit*. ENTJ math profs would tell their students to practice those algebra problems, and they could benefit from their own advice when it comes to understanding others' feelings.

At Work: If ENTJs want to maximize the effectiveness of their visions for the future, they would do well to consider other people's POVs, because ENTJs aren't going to accomplish their aims alone. Further, that saying about "two heads are better than one" is important. Different people bring different ideas and perspectives to the brainstorming sessions – perhaps they can bring something even the brilliant ENTJ didn't consider.

27. Can be forceful about their opinions

Positive: ENTJs stand up for themselves, that's for sure. Unlike Introverts, who are more apt to slide away from confrontation, ENTJs dig in their heels and get ready for a long session of back and forth – most of which is this personality type expressing why their opinion is the right one, period. Would that we could all be so confident.

Negative: One of the quickest way to lose friends is to always insist on being right. ENTJs get to their high places by being forceful and outgoing, but outside of work they can be viewed as pushy and rude, and may find themselves black-balled from groups where they were once welcome.

In Relationships: There really is no more entertaining sight than the ENTJ arguing with his or her partner about who is right. Best of all if the sassy mate can hold his or her own, besting the ENTJ with a flawlessly logical argument that leaves them, for once in their lives, speechless. The truth is, though, the ENTJ wouldn't have anyone else by their side.

At Work: At least in the workplace the ENTJ's knack for forceful opinions has the chance to be well-received. Since they tend to work in fields that value logic – a finite concept, unlike feelings – they can be more confident that their opinions on a matter are quite accurate.

28. Comes across as intimidating and overbearing

Positive: If anyone knows how to use intimidation to their advantage, it is the ENTJ. They are normally flawlessly turned out in their daily lives, giving off an air of wealth and success (even if they're just faking it for now), with a palpable confidence that shows they run this town – everyone else just lives in it. That kind of aura opens doors and opportunities.

Negative: If people are too frightened to talk to you, because your reputation precedes you, that can lead to some closed doors and missed opportunities – and ENTJs are all about opportunity and the possibilities of the future. They must find a balance between being respected and admired and being regarded as a cold-hearted control-freak.

In Relationships: As long as the ENTJ's partner has a will of his or her own, they should be fine standing up to their mate. This type will always have a soft spot and even a softer side that they will show to the people they love, especially if that person has earned their trust and loyalty.

At Work: In the workplace arena, however, the ENTJ may milk his or her reputation for all it's worth – after all, if you can get what you want without even having to lift a finger, why wouldn't you? ENTJs are hard workers, but the hallmark of this type is to work smarter, not harder.

29. Opportunistic

Positive: If an opportunity opens up to the ENTJ, whether it's a job or a really good deal on a nice mattress, they reach out and snatch it up. With their good sense of logic and reason, which they can employ in a matter of seconds, it is easy for them to quickly assess the advantages of an opportunity.

Negative: Rarely, ENTJs can be wrong, and even if it is a rare occurrence, they can sometimes fail spectacularly. Then, there's the fact that this type is less likely to stop and consider the ramifications of their actions for others, and if their opportunism is exposed, it can make them deeply unpopular.

In Relationships: Whereas the Feeling types might not even consider dating a friend's ex, the ENTJ is a bit more flexible on those types of matters. So if someone they are really interested in suddenly becomes available, despite the fact that their most recent break-up was with a pal, there is a good chance the ENTJ will move in.

At Work: Again, like so many of the other traits the brilliant ENTJ possesses, opportunism might not be so great around one's family, but in the workplace it can be the key to success. ENTJs aren't concerned about stepping on other people's toes when they jump at chances, but over time they should perhaps learn a degree of caution.

30. Enjoys debating with others

Positive: Though not so combative as the ENTP, who loves a good debate just for the heck of it and will argue the opposite of anything someone else brings up, the ENTJ likes to sharpen his or her wits on topics which touch their own beliefs. This type of situation can be good for the ENTJ, who despite believing in his or her own righteousness can nonetheless learn about a different POV.

Negative: One of the reasons ENTJs like to debate is because it gives them the opportunity to show off how intelligent they are (which is formidably) and to possibly make someone else look foolish. Not exactly the most compelling reasons to start up with someone, especially since ENTJs can "go there" with friends and end up damaging something really good.

In Relationships: If you can't stand up for yourself with the ENTJ, they are not probably going to be attracted to you. The significant others who can hold their own, who can intelligently and logically support an argument, perhaps even best the ENTJ in debate, is the lively, vivacious and similarly forceful person they want to be with. Make no mistake, pushovers don't appeal to ENTJs, not even ones who would do whatever they ask and cater to their every whim.

At Work: If ENTJs are "debating" at work, it's at least partially because they want to draw the best opinions and ideas out of their coworkers or subordinates. Further, those who aspire to be like the ENTJ in power can use this opportunity to impress their higher-up with conviction and intelligence that matches the ENTJ's own.

31. Enjoys lifelong learning

Positive: For as sure as they are that they are right in all cases, the ENTJ is nonetheless a devoted lifelong learner, whether they are reading the latest biography of the world's most wealthy self-starter or even taking online classes to gain a new skill. If anything, ENTJs view continuous education as further evidence of their intellectual superiority, because only a foolish man assumes he knows everything.

Negative: Still, it does give ENTJs a kind of intellectual superiority complex over everyone else, and that can be very off-putting. They might brag about how they took a seminar on leadership and ended up practically teaching the course themselves after the lecturer was proved to be "ineffective and idiotic." Perhaps their minions would be impressed with such a tale, but casual acquaintances are going to secretly roll their eyes.

In Relationships: If there is one way to engage the ENTJ, it is to challenge them to do something they have never done before and bet them that they can't do it perfectly in a given time. This can be a lot of fun for couples with a competitive nature, and they might learn to roll sushi together or go white-water rafting on a thrilling portion of river.

At Work: The ENTJ is confident in his or her skills, but underneath the skin they know, perhaps most importantly, what they don't know. And they want to remedy that as they go about taking over the world (the ENTJ's most favorite hobby-turned-career), so they broaden their horizons and their learning with a thirst for new knowledge.

32. Has clear and concise communication skills

Positive: This personality type always knows how to get their point across and leave no one in doubt as to their meaning. In a world that has grown mealy-mouthed, the ENTJ is a breath of fresh air, imbuing their environments – and the universe at large – with the honesty that is lacking in so many conversations. It is actually quite a credit to the ENTJ that they can say things that need to be said, even to family and friends.

Negative: For all their good intentions ("good" meaning that the ENTJ doesn't believe in lying or mincing words so as to confuse a person), ENTJs can be awfully rude and inconsiderate when it comes to the things they say. And they don't discriminate, not even in family situations. It is a positive when someone finally calls out the baby sister for being a brat, but the ENTJ is equally likely to tell his or her best friend that a pair of pants make their butt look huge. Learnt to filter, ENTJ.

In Relationships: Like other Thinking types, the ENTJ might not always be able to understand their partner's feelings, but they are at least honest about how confused the situation makes them. And ENTJs in the beginning of a relationship are not the type to play games, either; if they don't see the partnership going anywhere, they will say so, cut ties and move on.

At Work: The people who give a command couched as a vague request are no leaders at all, and they shouldn't be surprised when they are supplanted by another. That other could very likely be an ENTJ, who will even say the most unpopular things without trying to hide their true intent. But they make such effective leaders because they issue their desires concisely, so that people know exactly what they need to do.

33. Likes to have nice things

Positive: There is nothing wrong with liking nice things, especially not for the ENTJ, who works insanely hard to be afford to buy the top-of-the-line stuff. When someone spends as much time on their careers as the ENTJs do, it helps to remind them why they spend hours at the office if they can drive their luxurious vehicle and come home to a beautiful residence filled with things that they purchased cash, not credit.

Negative: ENTJs, if they are not careful, can fall victim to a certain degree of elitism, snobbery and materialism. There is a terrible gap between this nation's rich and poor, and ENTJs can often be found in the one percent at the top, living large because they are exploiting the working class. Hopefully ENTJs remember, when they are buying Louis Vuitton luggage or Chanel dog collars for their pampered purebred pup, to give back generously.

In Relationships: The partners of ENTJs may find themselves lavished with gifts, and it's enough to turn anyone's head, but rest assured, despite the flux of expensive tokens of their affection, the ENTJ has no qualms about pushing someone off the gravy train if there is no true connection. And because of their way with words, this personality type leaves no room for interpretation when it's over.

At Work: Work is very important to the ENTJ love of material items, because it's where the money comes from! For the ENTJ, a show of nice things is just part of the climb, and they might think of a nice luxury vehicle just outside of their price range as an investment, so that when they roll up to the golf course to play 18 with a guy they need to impress, the car speaks volumes and for once, they don't have to.